the
small adobe house

Agnesa Reeve

Photographs by Robert Reck

GIBBS·SMITH
P
PUBLISHER

salt lake city

First Edition
05 04 03 02 01 5 4 3 2 1

Published by
Gibbs Smith, Publisher
PO Box 667
Layton, UT 84041
Orders: 1-800-748-5439
www.gibbs-smith.com

Designed and produced by Kurt Wahlner, Venice, CA
Printed and bound in Hong Kong

Library of Congress Cataloging-in-Publication Data

Reeve, Agnesa.
  The small adobe house / text by Agnesa Reeve ; photographs
by Robert Reck.—1st ed.
          p. cm.
  ISBN 1-58685-065-2
1. Adobe houses—Southwest, New. 2. Building—Details. 3.
Pueblo architecture. I. Reck, R. (Robert) II. Title.
  TH4818.A3 R44 2001
  693'.22-dc21
                                                2001000862

contents

sheltered by the earth

A walled terrace provides a stage for the heroically restored Prof. James A. Wood House and its handsome Greek Revival entrance.

Facing, below: Built in the nineteenth century as an unadorned four-room adobe, this little house had been updated to Territorial style by 1899, when it was bought by James A. Wood, the new superintendent of the Santa Fe Schools. But by 1981, when this photograph was taken, it had fallen into bleak disrepair.

No one who does not live in an adobe house can imagine the bond that exists between house and resident. Walking into an adobe is like walking into welcoming arms. This is not just fantasy: adobe walls envelop you with a cool respite on a sweltering day and cozy warmth on a frigid one. The material itself provides these qualities, but the "look" of an adobe house—or one of the various looks—is also part of the welcome.

The yen to live in an adobe house can dominate lives and bank accounts. Traditionalists search, sometimes for years, to find old houses to reclaim. They sometimes pay very large sums for a house that is in such wretched condition that it must be all but torn down and put up again. On the other hand, lovers of the new enthusiastically adopt radical departures from

A cozy fireplace for winter and a cool patio for summer make any adobe house warm and welcoming.

classic design, and they, in turn, may search for years for the ideal site to erect an imaginative and startling edifice of adobe.

Do you live where it is practical to build with mud? In a surprisingly large area of the U.S. it is practical—in the Southwest and West where there is sufficiently light rainfall, less than twenty inches annually. There are also new technologies that add some substance, such as cement or asphalt, to the adobe bricks, increasing their resistance to moisture.

A popular, because usually much less expensive, alternative is the building of an apparently adobe house in some other material, such as frame or block or, for a certain period in New Mexico history, "penitentiary tile." (Pen tile was a building block manufactured by prisoners in the facility in Santa Fe at the time.) The substitutes can result in beautiful mansions, but they cannot embody the intrinsic integrity and comfort of adobe.

In some ways, remodeling an old adobe house is easier than building one of frame or other masonry, and the adobe process allows an artisan, whether do-it-yourself owner or hired worker, to express his talent in woodwork or sculpture. Although the results may occasionally approach the absurd, however the remodeling is done, it is virtually impossible for an adobe house to be without character.

In this book we have tried to express the charm and pleasure of working with adobe, both in traditional and modern ways, and to illustrate some of the many possibilities of this wonderful material. There are examples both remodeled and new, both classic and contemporary. Even a couple of anomalies in pen tile and conventional frame and stucco are included, illustrating the strong appeal of the adobe look.

Building or remodeling an adobe house is an artistic endeavor, with all the satisfaction, and occasional frustration, of any such effort. But once you live sheltered by adobe walls, you won't want anything else.

Built a few years ago for a woodworker, this little sculpture now offers charming living quarters.

Adobe construction is practical in the areas shaded on this map, except in mountain regions, which normally get more than twenty inches of rain annually. The dashed line demarcates areas unsuitable for adobe, and the southern Rio Grande area falls into this category. Although some houses there are called "adobe," most are, in fact, built of partly fired bricks or of local stone—either riverbank sandstone or caliche. (Map courtesy of New Mexico Bureau of Mines & Mineral Resources.)

from the
ground up
adobe's
long pedigree

imagine standing on a brushy riverbank, looking out over the empty plain and knowing you have to build a shelter using only what you see: earth, grass, and water. Given these few items, it is astonishing how much variety, beauty and, above all, comfort, man has managed to include in his shelter.

If you found yourself in canyon country, your choices were easier. In the canyons and rock escarpments of (present-day) northern Arizona and northern New Mexico, for example, large caves presented natural homes that could be enhanced with additional rock structures. Restricted space dictated that rooms be built on

There seems to be a special kinship between an adobe house and its surroundings. Sometimes the relationship involves a very private placita, and sometimes, as here, a magnificent panorama.

top of one another, anticipating the multi-storied structures at Taos and Acoma, and even modern apartment houses.

Inhabitants of flatlands had no such ready-made apartments. Confined to the available earth, brush, and water, they burrowed into the earth with pit houses—dugouts roofed with native twigs and brush covered by mud. If one used a cookie cutter to remove a pit house from within the earth and set it on the surface, it would be, in essence, a small adobe house.

At some point, the people of the arid Southwest developed a way of using mud as the material for walls above ground. The oldest known buildings of this type are the *Casas Grandes* of northern Sonora, Mexico, and near present Florence,

Arizona. In these cases, the adobe material, usually earth mixed with straw or grass and water, was built up into a vertical wall by adding hand-shaped bands of the mixture one on top of the other as the lower level dried, a method called "puddled adobe." Only after the Spanish arrived were forms employed to mold blocks in the manner still used today. Another earth-building method regaining favor is pisé, or rammed-earth, construction, where mud poured between rigid forms is compacted into sturdy, insulating walls.

Archaeology suggests the earliest adobe construction may have existed in the ancient Middle East. Certainly some pottery excavated in the area of old Persia and dated from the ninth to the seventh centuries B.C. proves that people of that region were skilled workers in mud. There is little doubt that adobe has been known since prehistory in every inhabited desert fringe, where extreme temperatures make adobe an ideal choice.

A model imported from Africa and the Middle East (a possible trend in its infancy), is the house of adobe brick with a vaulted or domed roof, also of adobe brick. It is suitable for quite arid climates, and the roof requires artisans with specialized skills.

Built low to the ground and immediately upon the street, this row of city residences hides its gardens in the rear. Shutters protect the residents' privacy while Guadalupe blue trim enlivens the façade.

The form of an adobe house—thick, soft-edged walls of usually no more than two stories—is dictated to some extent by the material. However, men's needs and tastes have wrought variations, from a windowless fortress to the vacation house with open expanses framing a mountain view, and from an unbroken line of contiguous city houses only a foot or two from the street to a tiny adobe house sitting alone in serene isolation.

In the more arid areas of the world, entire cites are built with no other type of structure, and in the southwestern United States, some dwellings of multiple adobe rooms have existed for almost a thousand years. Over the course of these hundreds of years, social as well as climatic influences have been brought to bear on the design of adobe structures. In the ancient cities of the Middle East, the desire to sequester his women as well as the need to provide protection from the intense heat influenced a man's design for his residence: high, windowless outside walls, leisure areas restricted to a private interior courtyard or rooftop, and ventilation and light only from those rooftops were common elements.

Almost infinite space insulates this small house.

The lack of windows onto a public area was also for protection from enemies. In the American Southwest, where multistoried community structures were built

starting in the thirteenth century, entrance was gained by a ladder leading to a second level, a ladder that could be drawn up in case of need. These large buildings, still in use at Taos and Acoma, consist of many small rooms on four or five levels, each level stepped back from the one just below, creating a series of terraces. The rooms serve as storage and sleeping areas, although most activity is conducted on the terraces or in the plaza below.

Doors were often made of ocotillo cactus ribs or slender posts; tiny windows, if covered at all, perhaps had a sheet of selenite, a type of translucent quartz. Floors, almost universally of dirt, sometimes were treated with ox blood, which dried to a glossy, hard finish.

Hispanic settlers did bring some reminders of home to enhance the plain interiors of the adobe house. In its usual state, the one or two rooms each had a fireplace (often of the corner type providing more heat with less wood), possibly a *banco* (built-in bench) built along one wall, and furnishings composed principally of blankets and skins. The Hispanic's home might have mirrors brought up the trail from Mexico, not for reflecting faces but to reflect light. An owner probably had some pottery from Europe, sometimes a silver spoon or cup, and occasionally

even a chair. (The *ricos* [wealthy] brought more, of course—a carved chest, even paintings.)

As the house was initially one room, there was no designated kitchen, and so, when weather permitted, cooking was done outdoors. The *horno*, the beehive-shaped baking oven of adobe bricks, sat near the house.

The few visitors to the American Southwest other than the Spanish in the early eighteenth century were transients—fur trappers and traders—with little or no interest in domestic architecture, and consequently having little or no effect on it. Only after Mexico achieved independence in 1821 and opened the region for trade with *norteamericanos* did newcomers arrive with any intention of building homes.

The inauguration of regular trade was of vast importance in home building. Besides terneplate (sections of metal roofing) and small panes of glass for windows, the Santa Fe Trail wagons hauled new ideas—and the occasional piano for a parlor. Metal tools became more readily available. Terneplate made possible pitched roofs for residents of mountain areas with some rain, and for those who felt the new roofline brought the prestige of being up-to-date. Glass brought light into previously dim interiors.

The horno is a beehive-shaped outdoor oven built of adobe. This example enhances an historic property of gallery owner Nedra Matteucci. A wood fire is built in the oven and burns until the horno is white inside. The ashes are cleared out before the baking begins. A Zuni cook explains, "After the fire is out, clean the ashes out of the oven with juniper branches. Then dip the branches in water and dab them on the floor of the oven. If the water drops boil and evaporate, the oven is ready."

The United States Army was responsible for the prevailing architectural influence of the mid to late nineteenth century. Although the Greek Revival style had been at its zenith in the East in the 1830s, it burst upon the Southwest in the 1850s as if it were totally new, chiefly because Greek Revival was the style favored for army posts. Structures were still built of adobe in most cases but now were adorned with white-painted trim, pedimented lintels, and doorways with sidelights and overlights. This ornamentation, coupled with a parapet topped by fired brick, became known as the New Mexico Territorial style. Its popularity has scarcely waned in the last 150 years.

Greek Revival details were not the only ones to be attached to the adobe house. With the arrival of the railroad in the late 1800s, a plethora of styles flooded into the region. All the fancy bric-a-brac associated with the Queen Anne fashion found its place on formerly plain mud walls;

To achieve Victorian elegance was the goal of this 1870s builder. The walls are adobe, but the emphasis is on a curved front veranda with fancy balustrade and brackets. The most popular treatment of a gable for these Queen Anne styles was shingle, whether the house was of brick, frame, or adobe. The shingles were arranged in any fanciful pattern that occurred to the shingler.

Italianate brackets sprouted from many a cornice; wraparound porches with turned balusters and spindle friezes replaced the traditional portal. In Arizona, the Anglo Territorial-style adornments were by no means confined to Greek Revival but embraced the range of new ideas.

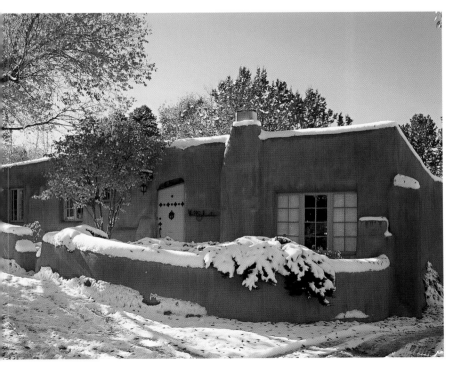

Facing: Nichos (recessed wall niches) display any object of beauty or interest. Commonly, they showcase a Madonna or other religious figure, as in this example from the J. Paul Taylor house in La Mesilla.

Will Shuster, credited with originating Zozobra (burning Old Man Gloom as part of the fall fiesta in Santa Fe) was one of the Cinco Pintores, a core group of the 1910s and '20s artists who influenced the Spanish Pueblo style in northern New Mexico. His house on Camino del Monte Sol displays a stucco with a somewhat art deco effect.

Starting about the turn of the twentieth century, these embellishments were scorned and discarded by an influential group of newcomers—artists, writers, archaeologists, and others of an intellectual bent. For the most part, these artists were poor, and simple, inexpensive little adobe houses suited them perfectly. Because they were outspoken about their preferences, and enjoyed the reputation of having good taste, the little adobe house became fashionable. Their houses had protected portals, but no arches (unlike the California Mission style), no large windows, and no windows within three feet of a corner.

The rules for interiors were unwritten but real. Walls were plastered adobe, with the heavy wood of lintels, sills, and doorframes exposed. Fireplaces could be parallel to a wall, but most often were the corner beehive shape with no mantels. A common detail was the *nicho*, a small niche carved into a wall to hold a *santo* (saint) or kachina figure.

The furniture and accessories were of natural materials—wood, wool, iron, animal skins—and were fashioned by hand. Boxy "Taos" chairs and couches could be put together by any moderately talented woodworker, and partly made up for their lack of comfort by being attractive and sturdy. The most favored decorative objects were Indian-made, but Mexican rugs and figures were also popular. Walls were either left the earth-tone color of the adobe plaster or were plastered in *tierra blanca* (white earth), with the lower half being covered in cloth to keep the mud plaster from rubbing off onto clothes. Curtains and other fabrics were usually bright colors. The atmosphere of these artist-inspired homes was simple, serene, and cheerful.

Homes by a group of builders of the 1970s to '90s, who proved to be artists in their field, offer a more sophisticated charm. These builders used the fluid lines of real adobe to construct homes that are sculptural. The lines of these houses flow in graceful curves, and the interior finish—the result of repeated and painstaking sanding and painting—is so exquisite that it invites sensual touch.

Whether the small adobe house is a work of art or a model of simplicity, it is by far the most appropriate house for the Southwest. The adobe serves as natural insulation, keeping the interior cool in summer and warm in winter, and muffling noise. No draft ever penetrates an adobe wall. The spaces of such a house accept with equal grace the basic curve of an Eames chair or the sumptuous gilding of Louis XIV. It is an easy house to live in.

It is also easy to reshape. You may incorporate all sorts of modern ideas and still keep the classic look of the small adobe house, affording enjoyment of the newest conveniences within an enveloping tradition. The advantages of working with an old adobe are both obvious and subtle. Obviously, the plain walls adapt to a variety of decorating styles, but old walls also have a mellow charm that adds an indefinable magic.

A varied outline and two portals make this house appear larger than it actually is. The vigas project in two directions because they extend into separate rooms with opposing dimensions.

from the top
roofs and ceilings

describing the classic adobe house brings up the same problem as describing the classic barbecue sauce—it all depends on what part of the country you are talking about. Barbecue sauce may be hot with jalapeños, or be thick and sweet, or have a vinegary tang, or offer countless other taste variations. In the same way, an adobe house may have sparkling white walls and a pitched red-tile roof, or earth-brown walls with vigas protruding from a flat roof, or it may even look like it was constructed of ordinary brick.

This kitchen/dining room shows a further option for a small residence with a gabled roof, an exposed-beam ceiling rising the full height of the gable. Using squared beams in place of vigas, with neat plaster between, creates a less-rustic effect. Edmund Boniface, architect.

The first adobe houses were mud boxes—square flat bottoms (no basements), four square flat walls, and a flat—or apparently flat—roof. The roofs should have an incline of one inch per ten feet of span in order to drain (though too often an inexperienced homebuilder neglected this). Though roofs were originally composed of poles, brush, and mud, tar-and-gravel has long been the accepted roofing material. In recent years, various plastics have gained popularity. One advantage of the tar roof was the ease of fixing leaks: all one had to do was haul a bucket of tar up to the roof.

The structure of the roof is apparent on the exterior because the major supporting members, the vigas, protrude through the walls. Most of these roofs have parapets, wall extensions higher than the roofs themselves, on all four sides. Wherever owners build their own houses, of course, there are interesting anomalies. For example, a nineteenth-century adobe on a ranch east of Laredo, Texas, has a parapet on the façade only, finished with a scroll at each end. In La Mesilla, New Mexico, a fat bumper-shaped pillow forms a parapet. Sometimes a

These hefty vigas were beginning to deteriorate, so the owners installed metal covers. Each cover extends over the end of the beam and is imbedded in the wall on the house side to prevent moisture wicking in from either end. The brick coping of the parapet typifies the New Mexico Territorial.

Shiny copper caps are not only decorative but also functional, protecting these vigas from water damage.

builder may fancy stepped corners, or curves at the center and each end. The most obvious style expression in a parapet comes from the addition of coping, or a brick cap, a principal characteristic of the New Mexico Territorial style. This coping, usually three or four rows of fired brick laid in a more-or-less intricate pattern, had its beginning as a protective cap for the vulnerable adobe wall. As Territorial style gained popularity, coping became one of the most visible elements of the style.

Roof drainage is directed to spouts called *canales* that pierce the parapet. They must extend out far enough so that water does not run down the wall, causing erosion. Canales differ according to neighborhood and the owner's preferences. In southern New Mexico they may simply be three- or four-inch metal pipes. In north-central New Mexico, where they are most often three-sided, metal-lined, wooden troughs open at the top, or hollowed-out round poles, decorative inclination may be to paint the interiors sky blue or, more expensively, line them with copper. In Texas and elsewhere, canales of carved stone or cast concrete may lend an occasional elegance.

Decorative blue picks out the pattern formed by two rows of canales, or rainspouts. These are probably capable of handling more rain than this New Mexico house will ever experience. The parapet illustrates a Spanish Pueblo version of the feature.

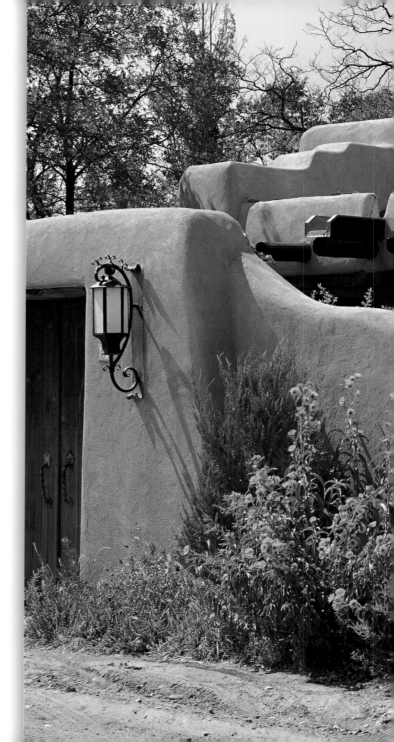

In the rural mountain villages of north-central New Mexico, the most common roofline is not flat but has a primary gable, with a secondary gable projecting to the front. A shed roof attached under the overhang of the long wing shelters the resulting portal. In many cases, however, an original flat roof is in place beneath the added gables, which became affordable after the arrival of the railroad. Much more practical than the flat design in areas where there is substantial rainfall, these gable roofs not only shed rain but, coupled with the adobe roof beneath, also afforded excellent insulation. The prevailing roofing material in these cases is

This sturdy canale is supported by a carved corbel.

metal, either corrugated or raised-seam, both relatively inexpensive and durable. Although sometimes left unpainted, these roofs more often brighten the landscape with colors such as a deep cobalt blue and reds ranging from apricot to wine.

The first houses in southern California were the same mud boxes as in Arizona and New Mexico, but they soon evolved in another direction, to what is known variously as Mission style, California style, Mission Revival, or even Mediterranean.

Early on, the Spanish missionaries and military forces on the California coast realized there was too much rain for flat mud roofs. As early as 1780 or '81, the residents of Mission San Antonio de Padua began firing barrel roof tiles, and since then, low-pitched red-tile roofs with

One of the attractions of rural northern New Mexico is the appearance of brightly painted raised-seam metal roofs on the L-shaped farmhouses.

29

earth-toned or white walls identify this elegant variation of the adobe house. For reasons not completely understood, barrel tiles have been rare in New Mexico and Arizona.

The earliest Texas residents in San Antonio, enjoying slightly more rainfall than those farther west, often thatched their pitched roofs with palmetto leaves or other suitable local grasses.

Climate dictated roof design in other areas of the country also, requiring substantial overhanging eaves in regions of high rainfall. In the mid-nineteenth century, a flurry of earth-building enthusiasm resulted in a number of adobe houses being built in seemingly unlikely places such as New York State. The appearance of these houses differed not at all from any other stuccoed, pitched-roof house in the neighborhood.

In addition to avoiding a leaky roof, owners were also possibly motivated by pride when they constructed a pitched roof over their adobe box, for an eastern or Anglo look was a great deal more fashionable in the decades after the railroad arrived in the Southwest.

These characteristic roof styles offered an intrinsic aesthetic bonus: they automatically created an individual and interesting ceiling on their underside.

Although uncommon in New Mexico except in the town of La Luz, where they were made by the La Luz Pottery for a time, the barrel-shaped clay-tile roof forms an important part of the adobe house vocabulary in California and Arizona.

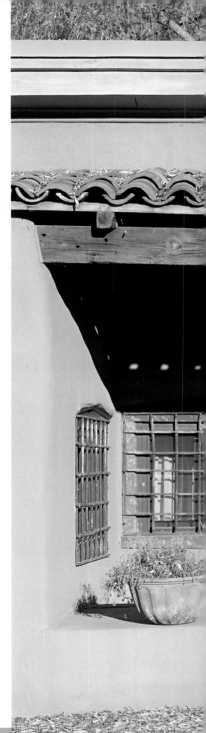

A few roofs employ a barrel-shaped metal tile that is less vulnerable to hail damage. It is usually painted "tile" red to enhance the illusion of clay.

The possible variations seem endless. Originally, the spaces between the vigas exposed *latillas*—thin, peeled saplings supported by the vigas and in their turn holding the brush-and-mud roof. If made of split cedar, they were *cedros*; in some areas they were made from the ribs of that useful building resource the ocotillo cactus.

Latillas, often laid in a herringbone pattern, give a charming rusticity to a room and are considered most desirable while being comparatively expensive. Because a roof of brush and mud tended to let dust sift down into the room, (or sometimes an insect with a poor sense of balance), housekeepers added a *manta*, fabric stretched beneath the vigas while wet and secured with a molding. When the manta dried, it pulled taut and formed a neat ceiling.

In modern days, the most common practice exposes the round, peeled logs—the vigas—in their natural color or stained somewhat darker, with flat boards above and visible in the spaces between the vigas. Occasionally, if an owner feels the ceiling seems oppressively low or dark, the vigas may be painted white.

Above: Because the roofs of early houses carried several inches of earth above the vigas and latillas, and sometimes because the vigas were installed before being fully cured, these members often acquired a distinct bow from the weight.

Endless ceiling variations are possible through the patterns in which vigas and latillas are placed. Latillas are often laid in a herringbone pattern, as on the facing page. Above the latillas to the left is a layer of carrizo (cane), but any suitable indigenous brush or reeds may be used.

Sometimes the weight of the original mud roof creates a graceful bow in the vigas. Flat or beaded boards between can be stained or painted white. Latillas are usually left a natural color but occasionally receive a "rainbow" treatment, with groups of three or four painted in contrasting colors. Often the boards are plastered. A recent custom, borrowed from other regions, curves the plaster between vigas, creating a distinctive coved appearance. A further innovation places skylights between vigas, especially in a long room or hall, apt to receive too little natural light.

Although the ceilings of some new adobes are raised to almost a two-story height, this produces a less-traditional effect than the customary eight- to ten-foot height. However, a few astute early homeowners realized a higher ceiling produced a cooler room, as did Oliver LaFarge in his Old Santa Fe Trail house in Santa Fe. Farther south in Mesilla, the builders of the 1850 J. Paul Taylor house raised the ceiling in the *sala*, the living room. Subsequent Anglo owners of the house removed the vigas and installed beaded ceilings in the reception rooms, probably following then-current fashion.

The supporting members, although classically left in the round, may be squared off into

A currently popular treatment of ceilings is to apply the plaster on a curve between the vigas, achieving a coved effect. Having a somewhat more finished appearance, it particularly suits this elegant bedroom. Cannon/Frank interior designers.

beams, giving a more finished effect than the rustic vigas. A creative builder may decorate a beam with a beading or brightly colored chisel border.

In churches or elaborate residences, the vigas are supported at each end by corbels, four- to eight-inch-thick wooden brackets extending from the wall along a foot or two of the bottom of the vigas. Builders, especially owner-builders, usually form the sturdy brackets into decorative curves and angles. Although related in function to the lacy brackets of Italianate or Victorian style, their character is much more robust.

Many portals, even on modest houses, display fanciful corbels. When a center beam is necessary to support the span of the portal, the upper beam load is spread by using a double corbel, carved at each end, sometimes called a *zapato* (literally "shoe" in Spanish.) Vigas and corbels visible on the exterior are left to weather or, more desirable from a preservation point of view, are stained a natural color.

When the metal roof was added to this portal, the builder chose not to bend the roof down to meet the existing vigas. Instead, he filled the gap with a fat bundle of latillas, giving the home a naturally rustic appearance.

inside out
doors and windows
floors and walls

One of the attractive features of a small adobe house is the close relationship between interior and exterior. The portal is the most readily apparent evidence of this association. Just as the roof dictates the ceiling design, so do the doors and windows contribute their special character to the interior.

Front doors invite guests to enter, but they also invite the artist to display all sorts of ingenious decoration. They often boast colorful painted patterns, applied moldings and medallions, and most often are hand carved in either simple or elaborate detail. Spanish Pueblo traditional doors do not have glass panes but are solid (or certainly solid-looking) wood. Sidelights and an over-door light characteristically embellish the door in the Territorial Greek Revival mode. Storm or screen doors may employ grilles of turned spindles both in upper and lower sections of the doors.

This entrance is enhanced not only by double carved doors and a mullioned overlight, but also by graceful small walls whose painted décor repeats their outline.

Another simple and distinctive feature of the Greek Revival style as adapted to an adobe house is the pediment, the triangular facing placed above the lintel of a window or door. Although sometimes built up with moldings and panels, a plain elongated triangle of wood often suffices as a clear statement of the style.

The first houses in the Southwest did not have doors opening onto the street. For safety reasons on the frontier, a home was entered through a *zaguán*, a heavy double wooden gate between wings of the house, reaching from roof to ground and large enough to allow a horse-drawn wagon to pass through. It was sometimes inset with a smaller, pedestrian door. The zaguán led to an inner courtyard enclosed by two or three portal-fronted wings of the house and by corral walls. Doors of the separate rooms opened onto the

When the U.S. Army began to build permanent posts in the Southwest in the last quarter of the nineteenth century, it introduced the popular Greek Revival style. This entrance is a beautiful example of the new fashion applied to an old adobe house.

courtyard. Usually the well was located here, and this area afforded protected outdoor living. Many modern front doors give a hint of a zaguán with their weight, decoration, and double leaves.

Rooms within the main living area often are not separated by doors, but by square or arched openings. In an old house, tall people will probably have to duck to avoid hitting their heads on the arch.

A classic Spanish Pueblo front portal and door are dramatized by a collection of Turkish olive jars. The slender hanging adorning the door adds a subtle Eastern touch.

Windows, too, still reflect their traditions. Set at the outside edge of thick adobe walls, their reveals may be paneled with applied moldings or simply plastered. Unlike the usually white plastered walls, wooden window frames may sport painted trim. The most popular hue for windows and doorframes is Guadalupe blue, as it is said to protect the inhabitants from the entry of evil spirits.

Windows may have no exterior facings, the stucco curving into the window frame itself. Often, the lintel, especially if it is a large beam (a robust 8 x 8, for example), is not covered over with exterior plaster, but is left exposed to display the nature of the structure.

Occasionally, a lucky homebuilder or remodeler will find a beautiful old door or set of windows to incorporate into an old or new structure. This was the case with the historic Donaciano Vigil House, which boasts elegant pedimented window and doorframes salvaged from a building on the St. Michael's College campus. The windows, made in the mid-1800s, were in a sad state of repair by 1960. By then, chatelaine Charlotte White says, "the windows were all broken and even some of the mullions. They needed a lot of work." The repairs were done and soon she recorded in her

Pediments showing the designer's allegiance to the Greek Revival vocabulary can range from finished renditions such as this to a simple triangular-topped board above an opening.

Although constructed by sculptor Boris Gilbertson in mid-twentieth century, this zaguán gate gives a faithful representation of the originals.

With one side enclosed, this former zaguán serves as a roomy portal facing the placita.

The graceful pattern in the brick paving of this zaguán exhibits the artist's touch.

journal, "How elegant and beautiful the windows look with all the whole pieces of glass. Never knew windows could be so exciting." Equally dramatic is a row of tall arched windows rescued from a church in El Paso and installed by the J. Paul Taylors in their large sitting room in La Mesilla, New Mexico.

Of course, today's practical considerations sometimes dictate aluminum window frames, but they usually are painted as if they were wood. One simple variation is to leave the heavy wood lintel of a window or interior door exposed, giving textural interest to the opening. For instance, the graceful scallops of a concha (shell), a favorite motif of colonial Spain, may form the top of a window, door, or nicho.

For the most authentic look, windows are multi-paned. (False mullions rarely achieve the proper effect.) In planning adobe homes, the artists of the twenties and thirties dictated that windows be small, no more than three feet square, and no less than three feet or so from a corner. Even this was a concession to contemporary taste, as the colonial period adobes had no windows except onto the courtyard, just as they had no doors otherwise. Because so much of adobe country has spectacular views, however, and the danger

The dining room of a redone c. 1912 house retains its vintage personality with a high window above the radiator and an open doorway where steps lead down to the living room. At the other end of the dining room are a corner fireplace and cozy seating area.

from enemy raids is considerably less, many home-owners opt to vary from tradition in this matter and use large paned windows to frame a beautiful outlook.

Either double-hung sash or casement windows suit an adobe house, and either interior or exterior shutters afford both privacy and light control. Interior shutters fold neatly against the reveals of deep-set windows. The Taylor house features a unique solution, with fabric gathered on slender iron frames that operate like shutters, opening against the reveals, or closing for privacy.

Louvered shutters are less common than panels, which may be perfectly plain or enhanced with molding. Decorative grilles of metal or turned-wood spindles, although not as common in the American

This doorway frames two lovely pictures: the garden close up and the mountain vista beyond. Jerry West, builder.

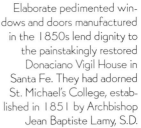

Elaborate pedimented windows and doors manufactured in the 1850s lend dignity to the painstakingly restored Donaciano Vigil House in Santa Fe. They had adorned St. Michael's College, established in 1851 by Archbishop Jean Baptiste Lamy, S.D.

A row of arched windows from an El Paso church provides ample light to a large, deep room in J. Paul Taylor's house.

Southwest as in Mexico, may adorn both windows and doors.

Choices for flooring in an adobe house are numerous and include mud, brick, tile, flagstone, concrete, and wood. Brick may be laid in any pattern, and even laid directly on sand without grouting by a certain technique. Tile, most popularly the large 12 x 12 inch Saltillo tile from Mexico, perhaps ranks as first choice in flooring materials, but brick and flagstone are also favorites. Concrete, expertly finished and coated, can give a dramatic effect. Wood flooring is easily installed and maintained or refinished, and it may be stained or painted. A Taos artist, for example, painted his wood floors in bright colors to good effect. Painted "rugs" adorn the floors of some talented residents.

Spanish Pueblo–style windows and doors often leave the heavy lintel exposed.

Because many adobe houses grow as the family grows—room by room or wing by wing—and tend to follow the contour of the land, they often have one or two steps between rooms, an idiosyncrasy that adds interest to a floor plan, if an occasional stumble.

In many small adobe houses a variety of coverings bring color and pattern to the usually neutral-toned floor. Mexican, New Mexican, and Indian rugs are possibly the most used, but elegant oriental and striking contemporary designs may be equally effective. Wall-to-wall carpeting (except perhaps in a bedroom) seems to be inconsistent with the adobe style and conceals the floor, a major decorating element.

Interior adobe walls are usually plastered, in textures ranging from rustically rough to porcelain smooth. An attractive though not terribly

The J. Paul Taylors contrived these metal-frame fabric interior shutters to control light and privacy.

Although few modern builders wish to be confined to small windows, they often compromise with tradition by using multipaned large openings.

practical use leaves the adobes unfinished, with golden flecks of straw or mica shining in the dried mud. Early settlers fastened a dado of fabric to the lower portion of such walls, and to *tierra blanca*, or whitewashed plastered walls, to protect the clothing of people leaning against them.

To begin with, of course, all adobe houses were plastered only with mud, outside as well as inside, but mud plaster must be renewed every year or two. Now very few houses are finished this way. Charlotte White says of the Vigil House that it is one of only three or four mud-plastered structures remaining in Santa Fe. Modern plastering techniques involve cement plaster.

A distinctive type of plaster decoration, *emborregado* has the virtue of adding interest without adding expense. The basic plaster starts with coarse texture. To achieve a border around windows, or perhaps a stripe across a façade, a pattern is then executed in the base plaster by smoothing wide bands of it. For example, twelve-inch-wide smooth bands add interest to the plain rectangle of a two-story building in Roma, Texas. A small adobe residence in Socorro, New Mexico, uses the same technique with smooth bands of white accenting gable and corners.

More popular than carpeting are vividly patterned and colored rugs. Whether Oriental, Mexican, Indian, or contemporary, they add life to any room. Doug McDowell, owner/builder.

al fresco
portals and other exterior features

Visitors to certain cities in the sunbelt are intrigued by the mysteries concealed behind high walls lining residential streets. Happily, when the visitor walks through the garden gate, he often finds the promise of discovery fulfilled.

The first thing to catch his attention is probably a roofed but otherwise open appendage to the house, a *portal*. The portal, which is a hallmark of the adobe style, differs from a front porch, back porch, piazza, veranda, or any other shelter attached to other styles of

Nothing is more pleasant for conversation or settling down with a good book than a portal like this one, sheltered but outdoors, and comfortably furnished. Superstition Mountain Golf and Club House, developer.

houses. In mild climates where air-conditioning is seldom necessary, the portal also provides the favorite setting for socializing throughout much of the year. Removable glass or plastic enclosures can make the utmost of this feature in winter, creating a room delightfully like a greenhouse. A side benefit is that the solar-heated air circulates through the entire house.

A portal lies directly on the ground and is not raised by a foundation, as most adobe houses themselves are not. Its usually flat-appearing roofline may extend from the main roof, or be attached just beneath the parapet. This roof is supported at eight- to ten-foot intervals by sturdy posts, which may be carved in a twist or other pattern, but more often are simple peeled logs whose corbels add decoration and support. Neither wood balustrades nor wrought iron is part of a portal. The white-painted, balustraded porches of some historic adobe buildings, such as El Zaguan in Santa Fe, are later embellishments inspired by Anglo ideas.

A portal's size varies in depth but traditionally extends the length of the house, preferably on the private, garden side, and facing south. Depth may be as narrow as six feet or as wide as twelve, but eight to ten feet provides a useful seating space. The small adobe houses of the 1920s and '30s tucked shorter portals in the L of the plan, affording a sheltered entrance but not much else. Bricks laid in various patterns or tiles of different shapes

This beautiful sweeping veranda typifies the best in the Victorian embellishments adapted to adobe homes.

El Zaguan, a historic Santa Fe structure, was built as a little two- or three-room Spanish Pueblo–style house. After 1879, when it was bought by prominent merchant James L. Johnson, it grew to a much larger residence with Anglo additions like this porch on the garden side.

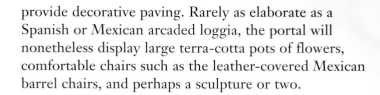

provide decorative paving. Rarely as elaborate as a Spanish or Mexican arcaded loggia, the portal will nonetheless display large terra-cotta pots of flowers, comfortable chairs such as the leather-covered Mexican barrel chairs, and perhaps a sculpture or two.

The protected wall of a portal is often painted white, to bring light into a deeply shaded area, with door and window surrounds outlined in the earth tone of the main house, or in Guadalupe blue.

An open door brings the beauty of the placita into a bedroom.

Living space of a small adobe home may be greatly increased or even doubled by an enclosed *placita*, or patio, open to the sky beyond the portal. If the brick or flagstone floor of the portal is simply extended, the result is a grand space that is particularly elegant when the placita surrounds a fountain or bed of flowers. Gardening in the placita is particularly satisfying because it is protected from wind and usually affords planting areas of both shade and sun. Plantings in the placita should include a generous proportion of evergreens so that it is never bare, even when the last chrysanthemum has faded.

Although few houses have the four wings necessary to form the traditional central placita of Spanish Colonial days (actually, houses of that size were by no means common, even then), many adobes are L- or U-shaped, requiring only one or two additional adobe walls to provide an outdoor space of utility and privacy.

Ideally, this courtyard adjoins the portal, which is available for shade and shelter when desired. Depending on the site and available landscaping, the garden walls may need to be six or eight feet high, almost as tall as the house walls, to give sufficient privacy. On a raised site, or with surrounding greenery, a four- or five-foot wall may suffice. This enclosure assures not only visual protection but also insulation from street noise.

For these purposes, a solid wall of adobe or stuccoed concrete block is most effective, but six-foot fences of thin, unpeeled cedar poles, called "coyote fences," blend with the vegetation and set off a house to advantage. When stone is available, it makes a handsome wall, especially laid up in "dry wall" fashion—that is, with no mortar apparent.

Snow outlines a graceful curve in this wall.

A rock retaining wall serves as the foundation for the adobe wall above.

Buttresses or serpentine curves add visual interest as well as support to a long solid wall. Adobe walls may be enhanced by brilliantly colored tile insets, particularly backing a lavabo, or small wall fountain.

Lighting giving the effects of firelight and candles is the most appropriate and charming for these outdoor rooms. Fortunately, ordinary bug lights put forth a warm orange glow when serving as lights on the portal. Outdoor fireplaces, both masonry and the portable iron type, give heat, light, and sometimes even cooking possibilities. Hurricane-shaded candles illuminate most al fresco dining tables.

The gate will be a focus of interest and artistry, applied with unlimited imagination. Designed to secure against intruders, the gate, like the front door, is usually built of solid wood. A decorative metal grille gives a lighter flavor of Old Mexico or Spain.

Another choice for the garden is a ramada. The ramada predates the portal in the Southwest, as it was in common use among the Indians of that region before any Europeans arrived. This structure consists of four vertical posts supporting a rectangular roof, originally of brush or cactus ribs and in modern times, either solid construction or lattice or other arbor construction as a frame for vines. It can be adjacent to the portal or perhaps the back door of the house, or stand alone in the garden, much as a gazebo might occupy a more formal arrangement.

Some gates bear the artistic expressions of their owners.

Colorful ceramic tiles are often embedded in the plaster of a wall, displaying the house numbers and, in this case, a decorative element.

Although no longer principally intended to deter coyotes, the tall coyote fence of unpeeled saplings is a dramatic reminder of the frontier. In fact, it is not unusual today (or tonight) to hear coyotes howl through the foothills and arroyos.

Especially where budget must be considered, the ramada offers an inexpensive and delightful solution for an outdoor haven.

Another type of light construction in the earliest days of the Southwest, and seen occasionally today, is the jacal. The execution of the pole-and-brush jacal varies widely from one area to another, ranging from any sort of temporary small hut in southern Arizona to a specific rectangular structure in Texas. It consists of small posts set either vertically or horizontally and lashed together with branches, the spaces being filled with mud. Sometimes mud plaster is applied over the entire structure. The roof is usually of brush supported by horizontal poles.

Still an inexpensive, quick, and easy building method, a few jacals are in use today. Fort Clark, Texas (no longer an active military base), has an extraordinarily well-maintained jacal mess hall built in 1854, and several original officers' quarters of stuccoed jacal are occupied by private families there. A jacal still stands on the historic property of gallery owner Nedra Matteucci, but these days, if you see one at all, it is most apt to be used as a garage or other outbuilding in a rural area.

Privacy and decoration are both provided by this handsome gate.

interior views
basics and frills

by its very nature, adobe allows a freedom of imagination and innovation unthinkable in any other building material. You can live in a sculpture of your own design, in an elegant, formal residence, or in a whimsical fantasy.

Small adobe houses often appear similar on their exteriors (at her first sight of Santa Fe, Mabel Dodge Luhan said they looked like barges on the Mississippi), but no two adobe interiors are identical. In the first place, the fact that the material can`be manipulated insures that it will be, and secondly, its resistance to perfectly straight lines precludes a geometrically regular house. Even the formally designed and furnished living room reflects the softening effect of adobe walls.

Early Hispanic homeowners often eliminated a number of

A Chippendale-style chair sits comfortably between an adobe fireplace and a banco, a wrought-iron lamp at its side.

subordinate or limited-use rooms, such as bedrooms or dining rooms, but when they could, they included a more spacious social room, or *sala*. An efficient way for the modern builder or remodeler to gain the effect of a sala, even within a small house, is to combine living, dining, and kitchen into a large proportion of the total square footage. For example, a house 30 x 30 feet could boast a sala 30 x 18 feet accommodating living, dining, and kitchen functions; two 12 x 10 foot bedrooms; a 10 x 10 foot bath; and a small connecting hall—all within 900 square feet.

One such simple little house, originally built about 1912, was one of the artists' houses that line Camino del Monte Sol in Santa Fe. This small house had its floor space enlarged in the 1920s and again in 1995. It encompasses all its changes gracefully, retaining both its early-twentieth-century character and its late-twentieth-century increments. Artist and interior designer Leni Schwartz Baxter, with her husband, historian John O. Baxter, planned the later changes including a modernized and expanded kitchen and a new studio. These alterations give the home a fresh and contemporary feel that harmonizes seamlessly with 1920s heat registers, fat metal doorknobs, and white-painted vigas. Because in the teens and twenties windows were typically small—for reasons of both fashion and practicality in cooling and heating—larger windows have replaced some of the originals. The floor plan, with moderate-sized rooms and several levels, is typical of a small adobe of the

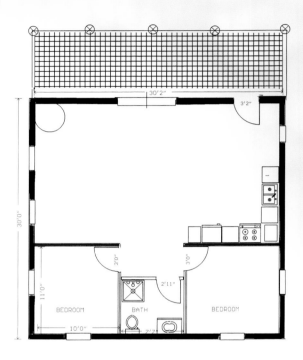

This little house hosts two bedrooms, a bath, and a generous kitchen-living room in less than 1,000 square feet.

Occupying the space formerly devoted to a back porch, this light and airy dining area affords the cook and guests a view of the terraced patio beyond. The plate cabinet at left is an eighteenth-century piece from New England.

earlier era, and the footprint of the house has not been changed. The new light-flooded dining area adjacent to the kitchen even occupies the space of the old back porch.

Because the Baxters are enthusiastic travelers and collectors, white-plastered adobe walls serve as blank canvases for carefully composed displays of exotic artwork, proving that intricate objects from the East—India, Malaysia, Indonesia—are one of the myriad choices for adornment in a house such as this one. Oriental rugs highlight the beautifully refinished original oak floors.

A radically different approach to remodeling was undertaken by Taos artist Dinah Worman. The rebuilt structure, the beginning of which was a 1960s ranch house, qualifies as trompe l'oeil because it is not adobe. About a third larger in scale than its models, it has the L shape and brightly colored standing-seam metal roof of the rural farmhouses that inspired it. While the

Contemporary furnishings blend smoothly with adobe walls and fireplace, spiced with exotic accent pieces.

contemporary interior bears no relation to even the '60s ranch style, the exterior remains true to traditional appearance.

In old and new residences, the living room focuses on the fireplace, which epitomizes adobe versatility. The design of the best adobe fireplaces, shallow with oval openings, provides a surprising amount of heat using the

Artist and traveler combine to produce fascinating collections. Each comb is beautiful, and the arrangement makes for striking wall décor.

Leni Schwartz Baxter designed her painting studio to fit inside the actual walls of the original garage. Ingenious planning, including impressive light arrangements, makes it pleasant and workable.

smallest amount of fuel. Usually three or five small logs arranged verti-cally against the back of the firebox are the most common fuel, although in some areas with access to coal, a diminutive coal grate may be substi-tuted. Sometimes a mantel of wood is installed, but more often the mantel is an adobe shelf, the protruding flue rising visibly above it. The hearth is usually quite low, only four or five inches high.

A variation particularly adapted to a bedroom or kitchen is a wood-storage space beneath the hearth, raising the hearth to a height of two or three feet. Storage spaces that are continuations of the adobe con-struction at the sides are also convenient.

This décor breaks the "rule" that small rooms should be painted light colors to create a feeling of openness. Light from the strategi-cally placed win-dows and from the traditional corner fireplace joins vivid color and pattern to warm this multipur-pose room.

Chairs by Marcel Breuer and a lithograph by Paul Sarkisian complement a minimal fireplace design.

Most of these fireplaces occupy a corner of the room, but there are exceptions. In order to form a corner on a straight wall, the builder may construct a stepped *"paredcito,"* a low spur wall at right angles to the main wall.

As graceful as it is useful, the small adobe fireplace deserves its place of honor and affection. In the Territorial style, reflecting the fashionable admiration for Anglo custom of the late nineteenth century, fireplaces are entirely different. Although their basic structure may still be of adobe, they usually are placed parallel on a wall and have a wood mantel of more or less finished design. Often, the surround is also of wood paneling, which may be further embellished with an inner surround of tile work. In a fireplace of this sort, logs for burning are placed in the parallel arrangement common to most of the U.S.

Natural and appropriate extensions of the hearth are *bancos,* built-in adobe benches on one or both sides. In early Hispanic homes where furniture was scarce, bancos served as seats. The built-in benches are excellent choices for small rooms, as they provide seating for less expense and in less space than other furniture. Bancos are popular on portals and along garden walls, as well.

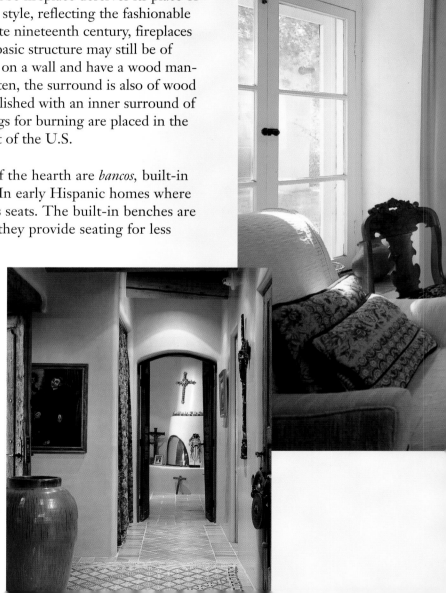

The nicho has a place in every room. It has a narrow flat bottom that serves as a shelf and usually an arched top for which the shell makes an especially beautiful decorative design. Sometimes used for practical storage, as in a kitchen, or for books, the nicho

A raised hearth gives prominence to the classic and stylish fogón (fireplace).

A bedroom with great distinction displays a row of figures above the bed in a nicho of a different shape. The fireplace, although of adobe, is parallel to the wall.

serves most often as a decorative element. It also may display ornaments of special significance, such as kachina dolls or santos. When fitted with doors, either solid or open work, the inset cabinet may be called an *alacena* (although that word more commonly refers to an independent piece of furniture, a small set of perhaps two shelves hung on a kitchen or dining room wall).

An adaptation of the nicho idea is the conversion of an unused doorway into a bookcase or shelves for kitchen utensils, perhaps. No floor space is lost, and interest and utility are gained.

Dining rooms suggest another built-in feature especially suitable for adobe construction: the buffet. With doors below for storage, and perhaps shelves above to display beautiful pottery, a waist-high buffet is attractive at all times and at dinnertime is a great convenience.

Furnishing the adobe house allows the owner the most exhilarating freedom of choice. For example, if you descend from five generations of Bostonians and are lucky enough to have inherited a goodly number of handsome antiques, your plain adobe walls will silhouette every graceful curve of walnut or mahogany without offering an obtrusive note. The delicate carving and cane of French Provincial may sit gracefully on an Aubusson rug beside an adobe fireplace.

At the other end of the spectrum, art galleries have for years imitated the simplicity of adobe rooms to accentuate their modern displays. They have long recognized its adaptability for the most vivid color and spectacular design. Most people have an eclectic assortment of furnishings—new, old, antique, and contemporary. In the Southwest the local styles are Mission and Taos furniture. They are handsome in a simple, boxy way and require a great many pillows to provide comfort.

The one piece of furniture that may be found in rooms of any décor is the *trastero*, a tall floor-standing wardrobe. There are beautiful and expensive antique trasteros, and less-expensive simpler ones, but each adds character to a room and because of its size is often used to balance the prominence of the fireplace.

Other popular items that blend well with a variety of styles of furnishings are chests—large old grain chests, painted antique traveling chests, new carved or plain Mexican chests—some evolved into a bench with back and arms.

Almost the only mistake made in furnishing the small adobe house is filling it so full of things that the serenity of the structure is obscured.

Thick adobe walls make it possible to carve indentations for shelves, nichos, and, when doors are attached, alacenas. This alacena is fitted with paneled doors and has bancos beneath.

The depth of the wall is ideal for open shelving, as in this case.

Facing: This dining room presents a large but simple, unadorned mantel.

innovations
large
and small

an adobe house has an endearing habit of taking on the personality of its owners. It does not dictate a way of life, but gently supports that of its inhabitants. Walking into someone's adobe home introduces you to the people as well as the house. Individual nuances meld comfortably into this ancient technique, even quite unusual ideas.

For example, Robert and Valerie Arber chose a unique centerpiece for their house—a Ping-Pong table. From

An industrial alternating-tread stairway by Lapeyre, leading to the loft, occupies much less space than a conventional stairway and introduces a visual fillip. The painting underneath the stairs is Red, by Florence Pierce.

The boundary lines of the Ping-Pong table echo a series of woodblock prints by Donald Judd.

the beginning, they planned that the table would be the dominant feature of their big center room when they built their new home south of Santa Fe. The table is not the most striking aspect of their home, however. The structure itself is the attention-getter. It is composed of two-story-high adobe walls supported by steel beams.

From the exterior, this home could almost be a traditional gable-roofed house in rural northern New Mexico,

although its single dormer near one end of the house flouts the more usual symmetry. A rectangle with a steep-pitched roof, its portal runs the full length of the structure. Gravel of the ample parking area extends into the portal and up to the house walls, meaning that a visitor has entered living space as soon as he gets out of his car.

As arresting as the exterior is, the drama increases as one enters the house. Exposed steel beams rise to a peak

In addition to providing room to maneuver in a game of Ping-Pong, this generous space provides for kitchen appurtenances, an office corner, and space for an extraordinary collection of martini shakers high on a shelf, out of danger.

On the T-shaped wall separating the small and large living areas is TV Clowns, a lithograph by Bruce Nauman, and beneath is Robert Arber's motorcycle, an MV Agusta F45, a model that starred in a recent Guggenheim motorcycle exhibition.

high above; a T-shaped wall to the right defines a small sitting room with loft above; counters to the left enclose the kitchen paraphernalia. Of course, there is the Ping-Pong table placed in the center of the large room, with maneuvering space all around for anyone bent on a championship match. An office is tucked in a corner behind steel cabinets and bookcases. This ample room is flooded with light from windows on both the east and west, and is enlivened by colorful works of contemporary art.

In the bedroom, windows are of two types: clerestory—a row of moderate-sized squares placed high on the wall, providing light and privacy—and two wall windows of usual proportion and position. Underscoring the black-and-white drama of the room is a concrete floor with a swirling design in gray and black achieved through a heat process.

Other arresting details are the industrial steel alternating-tread stairway to the loft and a bathroom counter that glows in the dark. Overall, this adobe house gives a view to the future but retains the virtues of adobe. As Robert Arber remarked, "You can't believe the difference in temperature when you come inside these adobe walls."

At the other end of the size spectrum is a house with only 820 square feet, designed by Archaeo Architects. Several elements, including an ample terrace with a large barbecue forming part of its wall, make the house feel bigger than it is. The terrace sits a level below the house, which occupies a wedge of an east mountainside with stunning views.

Facing: Totally simple without being austere, this black, white, and gray bedroom is, above all, serene. Clerestory windows (not seen in this photo) add light but do not deny privacy. The unpainted walls owe their luster to hard-troweled, diamond-finish plaster.

The beautiful, swirling design of this concrete floor is a perfect complement to adobe walls. The floor decoration method has to do with heat produced by a steel-bladed power trowel, employed at exactly the right stage of curing.

Above and right: Two interior views of the small house by Archaeo Architects, demonstrating the striking effect of brilliant color.

This cantilevered hearth appears to use no floor space.

The terrace and the other exterior concrete surfaces have a copper-toned concrete stain and a light broom finish. The interior concrete floors are the same warm color, with a polished finish. The living room also has a high-beamed ceiling with a thin whitewash that reflects light from large windows capturing the views.

An interior design of angles gives a spacious feeling within what is not, in fact, a large area. The triangular cantilevered hearth does not occupy any floor space. One end of the living room opens to the south with French doors; the other end is defined by what the architect calls a "free floating pantry," a four-foot-wide rectangular cabinet. It is plastered, as are all the interior walls, and set at an angle that forms a front entry on one side and faces the kitchen on the other. This pantry falls short of reaching the ceiling, allowing another visual escape that creates an illusion of space.

One particularly appealing and somewhat surreal feature in the Archaeo Architects design is a single arcade wall extending thirty feet to the south from the façade. The arches of this wall bring visual control and perspective to what could be an unwieldy forty-mile view spiked with 10,000-foot peaks.

An even smaller adobe by architect John Barton, about 700 square feet, carries such distinguished details that it has unusual dignity: molded copper cornice weathered to a rich bronze color, buff flagstone blocks serving as capitals and bases of the portal columns, an intricate brick pattern in the kitchen-foyer hallway—all within an intriguing complex of rectangular masses. Nothing is startling about this little house but its exceptional quality, yet all is fresh.

One sparkling new approach to the small adobe house is the use of color on the exterior. In Mexico, entire

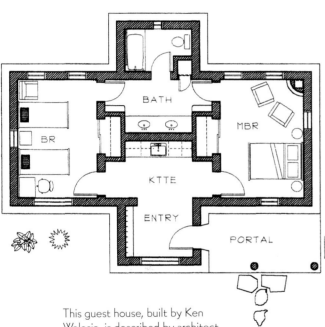

Very small but special, this less-than-700-square-foot guest house near Taos has exceptional detail and intriguing outlines.

This guest house, built by Ken Wolosin, is described by architect John Barton as "intended to work as an ancillary space to the main house. The [owners] wanted their [guests] to be comfortable, but to have meals and gatherings in the main house nearby."

houses have long appeared in brilliant or pastel shades of turquoise and pink or yellow, but the Southwest has favored earth tones. (In fact the historical ordinance in Santa Fe has required those tones.) The small adobes in the old convent district in Tucson have lately blossomed into little patches of bright color, including lavender.

In New Mexico, color may appear principally on windows, doors, and portals, most often in blue or turquoise. However, bolder hues do catch the eye on occasion.

The final word on the small adobe house is that it combines the best of several elements—comfort, adaptability, and tradition—and has almost limitless possibilities for expansion and personal expression.

Bright hues are blossoming in an old Tucson neighborhood, demonstrating a particularly cheerful way to spruce up an existing house.

This historic adobe in Taos, built about 1917 and known locally as "the Territorial," gets a lift with new, shiny turquoise paint on its portal.

resources

We have not bought goods or sought advice personally from all those listed below, but at the time of this writing, each of them offers an attractive collection, or original ideas, from which to choose.

furniture & accessories

Anahita
312 Sandoval
Santa Fe, NM 87501
505.820.2323 or toll free 888.666.2348
www.anahitagallery.com
Antique and ethnic furniture, architectural wood.

Antique Warehouse
530 S Guadalupe
Santa Fe, NM 87501
505.984.1159; fax 505.986.0789
Antique and southwestern doors, shutters, gates.

Artesanos Imports
222 Galisteo
Santa Fe, NM 87501
505.983.1743; fax 505.982.0860
Cataloges available: Mexican pottery, furniture, accessories.

Galisteo Home Furnishings
132 E Marcy St
Santa Fe, NM 87501
505.992.3300

Jackalope
2820 Cerrillos Rd
Santa Fe, NM 87505
505.471.8539

Highway 44 at the Rio Grande
Bernalillo, NM 87004
505.867.9813

12450 South Parker Rd
Parker, CO 80134
303.805.7687
Everything Mexican and Central American, from furniture and rugs to baskets and pottery.

La Puerta
1302 Cerrillos Rd
Santa Fe, NM 87501
505.984.8164 or toll free 800.984.8164
505.986.5838 fax
Architectural antiques, doors, shutters.

Ortegas de Chimayo Weaving Shop
Plaza del Cerro
Chimayo, NM 87522
Rugs, blankets.

Packards
125 W San Francisco St
Santa Fe, NM 87501
505.986.6089; fax 505.986.6158

Primativa
PO Box 161
Cerrillos, NM 87010
2860 Main St
Madrid, NM 87010
505.471.7904; fax 505.471.8952
Furniture, pottery, local crafts.

Ron Messick Fine Art
600 Canyon Rd
Santa Fe, NM 87501
505.983.9533; fax 505.983.1454
Morafine@earthlink.net
Antique Mexican and southwestern architectural details, furniture, and accessories.

Shidoni Foundry and Gallery
PO Box 250
Tesuque, NM 87574
505.988.8001
Sculpture, fountains, jewelry.

Southwest Spanish Craftsmen
PO Box 1805 Guadalupe Station
Santa Fe, NM 87504
328 S Guadalupe
Santa Fe, NM 87501
505.982.1767
Catalog $5. Furniture custom made in the USA.

Taos Furniture
1807 2nd St, Ste #100
Second Street Studios
Santa Fe, NM 87505
505.988.1229
Southwestern style, catalog and custom orders.

galleries

Cline Fine Art Gallery
26 Canyon Rd
Santa Fe, NM 87501
505.982.5328

Nedra Matteucci Galleries
1075 Paseo de Peralta
Santa Fe, NM 87501
505.982.4631; fax 505.984.0199
www.matteucci.com

Gerald Peters Gallery
1011 Paseo de Peralta
Santa Fe, NM 87501
505.954.5700; fax 505.954.5754

Wadle Gallery
128 W Palace
Santa Fe, NM 87501
505.983.9219

architects, builders & interior designers

Archaeo Architects
1519 Upper Canyon Rd, Ste D
Santa Fe, NM 87501
505.820.7200

John Barton (architect)
PO Box 195
Ojo Caliente, NM 87549
505.583.2429

Edmund Boniface (architect, 23)
Boniface + Associates
PO Box 1032
Santa Fe, NM 87504-1032
505.983.5266

Cannon/Frank (interior designers, 21, 35, 74)
340 W Diversey Pkwy #2518
Chicago, IL 60657
773.327.4099

Conron & Woods (architects)
1807 2nd St
Santa Fe, NM 87505
505.983.6948

Doug McDowell
McDowell Construction
433 W San Francisco St
Santa Fe, NM 87501
505.982.5238

Beverley Spears
Spears Architects, AIA
1334 Pacheco
Santa Fe, NM 87501
505.983.6966

Superstition Mountain Golf & Club House
(developer, 54)
8000 E Club Village Dr
Superstition Mountain, AZ 85219-9985
480.983.3400

Jerry West (builder of details, 48, 66, 76)
Blue Raven
Santa Fe, NM 87501
505.424.3959

landscaping

Plants of the Southwest
Agua Fria
Rt 6, Box 11A
Santa Fe, NM 87501
505.438.8888

building materials

Adobe Man
1627 C de Baca Ln
Santa Fe, NM 87505
505.986.3995

Captain Marble
1208 Cerrillos
Santa Fe, NM 87501
505.982.0276
Variety of marble, stone.

Hansen Lumber Company
1113 Calle Largo
Santa Fe, NM 87501
505.471.8280; fax 505.473.4633
Vigas, latillas, beams, corbels.

Paul Zimmerman
Frontier Wood
4523 Hwy 14
Santa Fe, NM 87505
505.474.9663
Reclaimed old-growth timbers.

magazines

El Palacio
The Magazine of the Museum of New Mexico
228 East Palace Ave
Santa Fe, NM 87501
505.827.6454

New Mexico Magazine
Subscriptions PO Box 12002
Santa Fe, NM 87504
800.898.6639

Preservation Magazine
The Magazine of the National Trust for
Historic Preservation
1785 Massachusetts Ave NW
Washington, DC 20036
800.944.6847

Santa Fean
444 Galisteo
Santa Fe, NM 87501
505.983.1444; fax 505.983.1555
800.770.6326

books

Bunting, Bainbridge. *Early New Mexico
Architecture*. Albuquerque: University of New
Mexico Press, 1976.

————. *Taos Adobes*. Santa Fe: Fort Burgwin
Research Center, Museum of New Mexico
Press, 1964.

McHenry, Paul Graham. *Adobe: Build It
Yourself*. Rev. ed. Tucson: University of Arizona
Press, 1985.

Santa Fe Historical Foundation. *Old Santa Fe
Today*. Fourth ed. Albuquerque: Published for
The Historic Santa Fe Foundation by the
University of New Mexico Press, 1991.

websites

www.earthbuilding.com
www.tsha.utexas.edu/handbook/online/
http://nmculturenet.org
www.trulytexan.com
www.newmexicostyle.com

acknowledgments

Obviously, this book could not exist without the help of the owners of the houses we visited and photographed. Their hospitality and welcome made the project a real pleasure, and we thank them profoundly. Some of their names are mentioned, and some preferred to remain anonymous, but we are grateful to all and enjoyed glimpses of them and their lives.

Major support came from John P. Conron, F.A.I.A, F.A.I.D., who lent his formidable store of knowledge to both research and editing. Our editor, Madge Baird, added encouragement and valuable suggestions.

Most of all, gratitude is due to Jack Reeve, who entered into the spirit of the project with total support, traveling hundreds of miles to look at hundreds of houses, and contributing to many hours of discussion with both patience and shrewd commentary.

—Agnesa Reeve

most photographers require the invaluable support of a good studio manager and first assistant, and the requirements for this project were no different. Mary Elkins, my business associate for more than sixteen years, performed both tasks with such accuracy and grace that without her mindful attention to detail and unfailing support, the project would not have moved so smoothly. Many thanks also to Matt Gray, whose good humor and assistance helped get things done while shooting on location.

—Robert Reck

index